Where?

Jane Belk Moncure • illustrated by Lois Axeman • cover and title page designed by Mina Gow McLean • created by The Child's World

 CHILDRENS PRESS, CHICAGO

Library of Congress Cataloging in Publication Data

Moncure, Jane Belk.
  Where.

  (Question books)
  Summary: Answers such questions as "Where does
chocolate come from" and "Where do chimpanzees sleep?"
  1. Questions and answers—Juvenile literature.
[1. Questions and answers]   I. Axeman, Lois, ill.
II. Title.   III. Series.
AG195.M623   1983   031'.02   83-7307
ISBN 0-516-06593-9

Where?

Where do the

Some raindrops splash into puddles—the kind you like to jump over!

Some raindrops drip down into the soft earth to water the roots of grass, flowers, and trees.

Some raindrops tumble into rivers. When it rains a lot, the raindrops may make a river overflow.

The sun shines and heats some tiny raindrops. It draws them back up into the sky. There they form a cloud, float over your head, and—oops!— rain down again!

raindrops go?

Where do tears

There are always tears in your eyes. They keep your eyeballs wet. As you blink your eyelids, the tears wash your eyes and keep them clean.

come from?

The tears are held in little sacs behind your eyelids. When you cry or laugh a giggly laugh, the tiny tears overflow. They overflow right out of your eyes and down your cheeks.

Don't you wish chocolate bars grew on trees? You could just pick a candy bar when you wanted! Well, chocolate does grow on trees. Just not in bars.

Chocolate is made from cacao beans. The beans are found inside pods. The pods grow on cacao trees.

chocolate come from?

But watch out! Don't eat the beans! They are very bitter. The beans must be dried, roasted, crushed, melted, and mixed with milk or sugar.

When all this is done, there is chocolate. Chocolate from trees.

The fuzzy caterpillar knows just where to go when it gets cold. He crawls into a stump or under a rock and rolls into a ball. There he spends the winter.

Maybe that is why he is nicknamed, "woolly bear!" Like a bear, he sleeps away the winter!

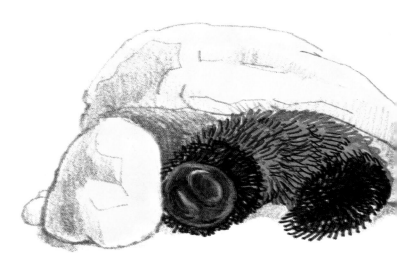

Other caterpillars spend the winter hanging in cocoons.

caterpillars go when it's cold?

Most caterpillars change into butterflies or moths long before it gets cold.

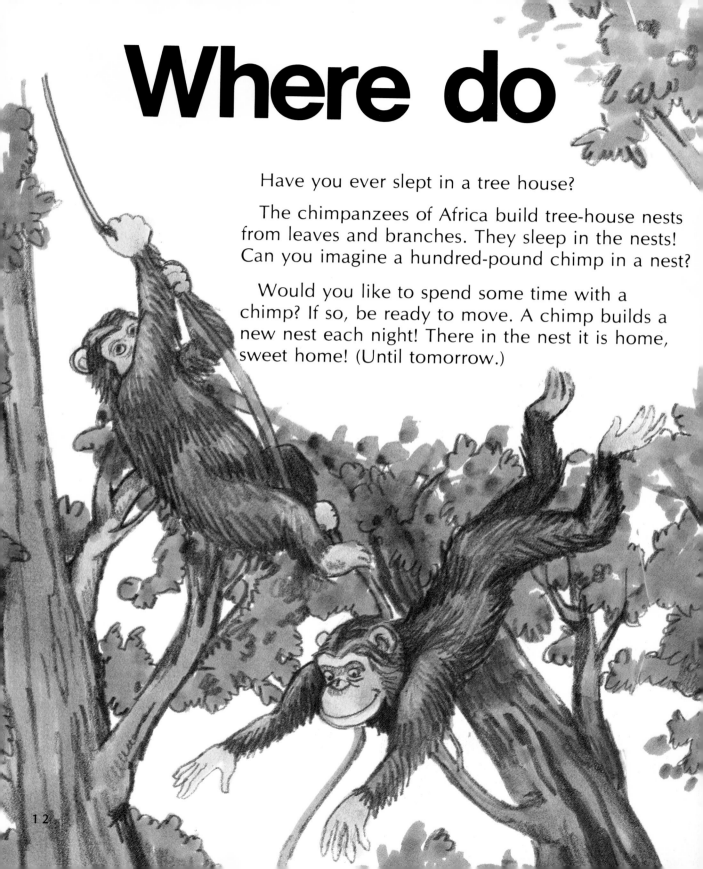

Where do

Have you ever slept in a tree house?

The chimpanzees of Africa build tree-house nests from leaves and branches. They sleep in the nests! Can you imagine a hundred-pound chimp in a nest?

Would you like to spend some time with a chimp? If so, be ready to move. A chimp builds a new nest each night! There in the nest it is home, sweet home! (Until tomorrow.)

chimpanzees sleep?

Where does

When you make a
valentine, thank a tree.

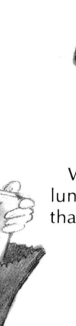

When you pack your
lunch in a paper bag,
thank a tree!

Whenever you use
paper, thank a tree! The
paper was once part of a
tree. Paper is made from
the wood of trees.

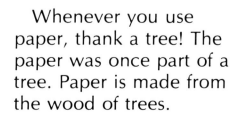

paper come from?

First the wood is ground into very small pieces.

Then it is put through many machines at a paper mill. It is washed, cooked, rolled, and pressed. It is turned into paper.

Paper is used for many things. Whenever you use it, thank a tree!

Where do frogs ice on the

Long before ice forms, frogs fatten themselves for the long winter ahead. Then they dig down into the mud at the bottom of the pond. There they settle into a kind of deep, deep sleep. It's called hibernation.

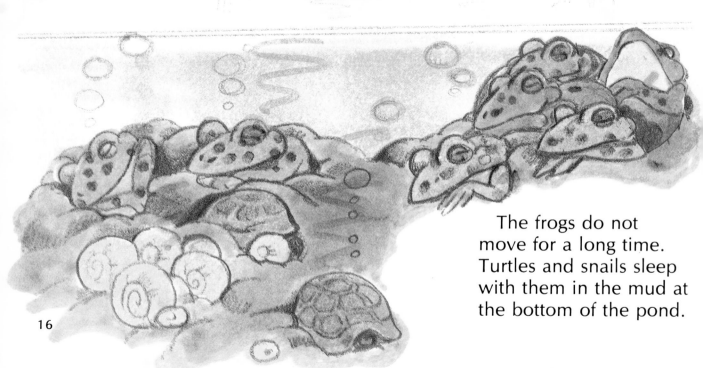

The frogs do not move for a long time. Turtles and snails sleep with them in the mud at the bottom of the pond.

16

go when there's pond?

When spring comes, the frogs are some of the first to swim to the water's edge. They croak as if to say, "Hi, spring!"

17

Where does a

Watch a squirrel scamper about with an acorn in her mouth. She may climb to her nest in the oak tree. Perhaps she will leave the acorn there.

She may dig a hole in the soft earth with her front paws and bury the acorn. Day after day, she scampers back and forth. She stores away food for winter.

squirrel hide her seeds?

The squirrel will never remember where she hid all those acorns and other seeds. She will find and eat many of them during the winter. But some will be left in the ground.

When spring comes, those seeds will sprout. New oak trees will grow!

The squirrel doesn't know it, but she is quite a farmer. She plants new trees every year!

Where do waves

On a very windy day, ocean waves will be high!
On a calm day, the ocean waves will be low.

Watch a wave reach the shore. The top of the
wave will roll over. It will spill into foamy bubbly
spray. Be careful; you might get wet!

come from?

Most waves are made when wind blows across the water. Wind pushes the water up into rolling hills.

The wind may make one wave after another for miles and miles.

Where do birds

Some birds stay in the dogwood tree in your backyard.

Some birds fly south! These birds fly across mountains, deserts, and even oceans. They fly in giant flocks . . .

. . . or in small groups . . .

or all alone.

go in wintertime?

Some birds fly by day. Some by night. They fly many places. They fly to Brazil, Mexico, and Peru.

The Arctic tern flies from the top of the world to the bottom of the world for his winter vacation!

Each spring, something tells the birds to come home again. And they do!

Where do

If you want to see where penguins live, hop on a jet plane! Be sure to take your warmest coat. If you "penguin watch" in Antarctica, you'll shiver. It's icy cold all year!

In their black and white feathers, penguins stay as warm as toast. They look like roly-poly dwarfs. They waddle on the ice as if playing "Follow the Leader."

penguins live?

Penguins are friendly. You can get quite close to them, for they do not fly. They only use their wings for swimming.

See for yourself. But if you can't fly to Antarctica, penguins also live on islands off Australia and New Zealand, too. Or try a visit to your nearest zoo.

25

Where do people

People get nicknames from other people. A red-headed boy may be nicknamed, "Red," by his best friends.

A little girl wants to call her big sister "Sugar." The word comes out "Tugar." From then on, big sister is nicknamed, "Tugar."

A boy wins a race. Someone nicknames him "Fast Eddie."

get nicknames?

Even presidents get nicknames. Long ago President Lincoln was nicknamed, "Honest Abe."

Using a nickname may be a way to show a person you like him. He is someone special.

What's your nickname?

Where do from?

Snowflakes come from the sky! They form when drops of water and bits of dust freeze into ice crystals in the clouds.

The snowflakes tumble together. Millions and billions of them fall to the ground. They make a blanket of snow.

If you could look at snowflakes under a microscope, you would see that each one has six sides. And each one is a different beautiful shape. A necklace of snowflakes would be fit for a queen!

snowflakes come

The next time you go walking in the snow, try to catch a snow jewel. Be quick! Before it becomes part of a snowbank.

A little road may wind around a bend to a farmhouse. It may stop there.

Or it could wind on around right into a bigger road. It could go over mountains to a small country town.

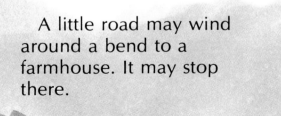

From town it might run right into a main highway. It could keep on going into a city somewhere miles ahead.

the road go?

In the city, the road could become a giant highway with eight lanes and tons of traffic zooming along.

Why, somewhere up ahead a little road could even become part of a super highway stretching for a thousand miles!

Some say the best way to know where the road goes is to follow it!